GOODNIGHT WORLD

written by
REBECCA PARKINSON

spck

illustrated by
PATRICK CORRIGAN

When God made the world, he looked down from above,

and he said, 'I'm so happy it all looks so good.

Each place and each country, the sea and the land.

All bursting with life and all held in my hands.'

And God made a promise to not turn away,

as day followed night and as night followed day.

He never would sleep but he'd watch from above,

as the world settled down, he would look down with love.

As darkness falls in the rainforests...

Goodnight little monkeys, stop swinging around,
cuddle down on the branches up high off the ground.

Goodnight resting sloths, hold on tight in the trees,

while the branches sway softly in the cool evening breeze.

Goodnight red-eyed frogs with your suction-cup toes,

cling on tight to the leaves as you drift off and doze.

Quieten down noisy birds, as the soft darkness falls.

Goodnight to the toucans and scarlet macaws.

As darkness falls
on the grasslands...

Goodnight sleepy elephants,
lie down on your sides
or nap as you lean on the trees
scattered wide.

Goodnight stripy zebras, in the dusk huddle near,

feeling safe from all danger, you can sleep without fear.

Goodnight tall giraffes,

check for predators first,

then with eyes still half open,

quietly sleep in short bursts.

Goodnight tired ostriches,
stretch out and yawn,
now that night-time has come,
you can rest until dawn.

As darkness falls in the deserts...

Goodnight dusty camels, as you kneel then lie down.

Let your eyes softly close as the sand swirls around.

Goodnight fennec fox, line your burrow to rest.

Your sharp ears alert to the kits in your nest.

Goodnight little lizards, as the temperature drops,
sleep hidden and warm in the sand and the rocks.

Goodnight to the meerkats, stop and rest for a while,

safe underground, you sleep in big cosy piles.

As darkness falls in the Arctic...

Goodnight polar bears, dig deep holes for your beds.

Use your soft furry paws as rests for your heads.

Goodnight weary walruses, sleep well in the dusk,

on the ice or in water, hanging on by your tusks.

Goodnight little penguins, in the freezing cold weather,

sleep well as you nap huddled closely together.

Goodnight sleepy seals, make a choice where to be,

you can sleep on the land or can sleep in the sea!

As darkness falls in the oceans...

Deep down in the oceans
with colours so bright,
it's tricky to see if it's
day or it's night.

Goodnight little fish, as you hover to rest,

keep your eyes open wide in the place you like best.

Goodnight to the whales, lined up far from the shore,

sleep safe with your tails pointing to the sea floor.

Goodnight sleepy turtles, so warm in your shells,

sleep silent and floating, in the place you know well.

As darkness falls across the world...

In fields, in forests, in jungles, on plains,

animals settle down for night-time again.

And children in homes become quiet at last,

as they climb into bed, now that day-time has passed.

And as we close our eyes, let us pause to decide

to do all that we can to keep each creature alive.

To protect all the wildlife, to treat the world right,

so the animals can settle to sleep every night.

Sleep tight animals...Goodnight.

Sleep peacefully tonight.

As darkness falls in my house...

I say my prayers and I close my eyes tight,

and if it's too dark, I will ask for a light.

And I know God is looking from heaven above.

And I know that I'm safe, as a child whom he loves.

So as I go to sleep, I know God stays awake,

watching over the world until morning breaks.

Goodnight world.

For Lucas,
with love x

First published in Great Britain in 2021

Society for Promoting Christian Knowledge
36 Causton Street, London SW1P 4ST
www.spck.org.uk

British Library Cataloguing-in-Publication Data
A catalogue record for this book is avaliable from the British Library

ISBN 978-0-281-08409-8

Printed in China by Imago

Produced on paper from sustainable forests